Let your light shine, Renee!

Mary Jane

# THE ART OF FIELDING QUESTIONS WITH FINESSE

## A Guide to Handling Difficult People, Sensitive Situations and Tough Questions

**Mary Jane Mapes**

**Kalamazoo, MI**

# What Others Have to Say...

*"It's great! This book is a real winner!"*

> Timothy Stack, CEO
> Borgess Medical Center

*"Packed with easy to understand, proven techniques, Mary Jane's guide to fielding questions is a powerful resource for presenters at all levels of experience. Use of the skills she describes will turn fear of questions into confidence, control and greater speaking effectiveness."*

> Timothy H. Bohrer, Vice President
> Technology
> James River Corporation

*"The difference between conducting a successful meeting and failure may depend on your ability to apply the concepts in this manuscript."*

> Roger Andrzejewski, Director
> Human Resources
> Lacks Enterprises, Inc.

*"Learning how to field questions in an open forum is a painful process and it often leads to damaging mistakes. The Art of Fielding Questions with Finesse will help many presenters avoid such mistakes through the use of specific how-to strategies."*

> Timothy Jenney, Superintendent
> Union Public Schools, Tulsa, OK

*"Straight-forward and to the point. The Art of Fielding Questions with Finesse should be must reading for anybody who deals with people in a public forum."*

> Patrick J. Nolan, Managing Partner
> Crowley, Olsman, Nolan & Berman, P.C.

*"This is the best and most comprehensive guide to answering questions I have ever read. I'd highly recommend it."*

> Brian Long, Ph.D., President
> Marketing and Management Institute, Inc.
> Author of *The Win/Win Negotiator*

*"Read this book again and again.  Every page is filled with ideas for improving your ability to build true dialog in a group situation."*

PETER HOEKSTRA, Member of Congress
2nd District, Michigan

*"Most audiences evaluate speakers by their ability to answer their questions. Mary Jane Mapes helps us  to do a common thing uncommonly well."*

RICHARD Y. ST. JOHN, Public Affairs Officer
Kalamazoo Foundation

*"This book takes the presenter past the skill of delivery.  The pearls Mary Jane  shares from her vast experience show how to cement the message through skillful handling of questions and objections. Putting these pearls into practice is a must for anyone who wants to become an effective communicator."*

H. A. VAN LUNENBURG, Director
Worldwide Sales & Marketing Training
The Upjohn Company

*"This is one of those books you keep reading over and over again. Every page is packed with great ideas."*

S. MARTIN TAYLOR, Vice President,
Community and Governmental Affairs
Detroit Edison

# THE ART OF FIELDING QUESTIONS WITH FINESSE

## A Guide to Handling Difficult People, Sensitive Situations and Tough Questions

**Mary Jane Mapes**

Kalamazoo, MI
USA

# Dedication

*This reference guide is dedicated to my clients
and to all who have participated in my communication
seminars throughout the United States
for providing me with the valuable insight needed to make
this guide to fielding questions so specifically
targeted and power-packed.*

# Foreword

Here is a slim volume that is truly loaded with cutting edge counsel for all who aspire to the mastery of interpersonal skills.

It is obvious that Mary Jane Mapes has "been there." The kind of insights and hands-on techniques provided here have clearly been honed and sharpened in the arena of much actual experience.

But perhaps the best part of all is that these techniques reflect a concern for the dignity and significance of people and truly aid in the enhancement and empowerment of others.

In my 36 years of speaking, consulting and training throughout the world, I have encountered tens of thousands of people who need and want this kind of guidance.

Read it again and again and you will grow and grow.

> *Joe D. Batten*
> *Chairman of the Board*
> *The Batten Group, Inc.*

# Table of Contents

Introduction                                                                    15

About this reference guide                                                      19

Why it is advisable to elicit questions and/or comments                         23

How to prepare for Q & A                                                        27

How to elicit questions                                                         31

The process for responding to questions                                        37

When to take questions                                                          43

Difficult People and Challenging Questions                                     47

    What to do when the question is unclear or vague        49

    How to avoid responding too quickly                     49

    What to do when the questioner speaks with a heavy accent   50
    or has poor language usage making it difficult for you to
    understand

    How to deliver a negative message in a positive way      50

    How to avoid engaging in dialogue with a member of the   51
    audience

    How to handle a comment that has nothing to do with your  51
    objective

    How to handle a question that will be answered later in your   52
    presentation

    What to do when the response needed is too involved for the   52
    majority of the audience

    How to handle a question covered in detail in your talk   53

    How to handle a question when you do not know the answer  53

    How to determine when you have given enough information   54

    How to handle a request for proprietary information       54

    How to handle a situation when you cannot answer a        54
    question and the questioner will not accept the fact that you
    do not have an answer

    How to handle a questioner whose personal experience      55
    refutes your facts

How to handle a response from a superior who provides incorrect information    55

How to handle a person who answers for others    56

How to handle a person who interprets for others    56

How to deal with a "funnel"...the person who serves as the mouthpiece for all others in attendance    57

How to respond to a "loaded" question    58

How to handle a complex question    58

How to handle a "What if" question    59

How to respond to a question that requires you to take a position with which you do not agree or a position which is not "politically correct"    59

How to answer when there is no "right or wrong" to the issue    60

How to avoid a gripe session    60

How to handle the "expert" who wants to editorialize    60

How to handle the "know-it-all"    61

How to handle a loud, disruptive detractor    62

How to handle someone who disagrees or who wants to discredit you or your information    62

How to handle an attack on the organization    65

How to handle a person who gives a "Yes, but" response to your response    66

How to deal with an angry person    66

How to handle a situation that appears to be getting out of control    68

How to handle an audience in conflict    69

How to regain control once you have lost the attention of the group    70

How to gracefully end a Q & A session    71

Summing up    73

# INTRODUCTION

Your pulse quickens, your eyelid twitches, your mind races. A stranger in the audience has just accused you and your company of intentionally lying to the public. How do you respond?

If you have ever faced an audience unprepared for their questions, you undoubtedly know the fear certain questions can ignite.

Through my work teaching executive speaking skills in hundreds of corporations and organizations, I have come in contact with many people from around the world, and continue to be impressed with their keen interest in what it takes to build a relationship with members of their audience. Many profess they spend hours working on a prepared presentation, only to find their hopes for a positive outcome dashed in the last twenty minutes of their meeting...the time most presenters devote to responding to questions from the audience. The fact that you are reading this book indicates that you can probably identify with their disappointment at falling short of the mark.

Why is it that so many people neglect to prepare for the question and answer session? The biggest reason given by most people is that their primary focus is on their prepared remarks. Handling questions is not perceived as a potential problem area for them. They figure they know their subject, and they can handle whatever comes their way. It is only when faced with a challenging question or a person who angrily disagrees, that they realize that they are inadequately prepared.

In this reference guide you will find eight topic areas.

In Section 1, you will find *"Information about this reference guide,"* which explains why interaction between you and the audience is important, and how this reference guide will be helpful to you.

In Section 2, *"Why is it advisable to elicit questions and/or comments from your audience?"* you will discover the hidden benefits of a well-handled question and answer session.

In Section 3, *"How do you prepare for Q & A?"* you will read about what one company did to improve its public image by being better prepared for questions, and the lessons they learned that you can adapt to your own use.

In Section 4, *"How do you elicit questions?"* you will discover the importance of setting a "question-friendly climate." You will learn a three-step approach to eliciting questions and comments that lets the audience know that you are sincere in your desire to address their questions. You will then find specific suggestions for eliciting questions and comments from your audience members if they are reluctant to respond to your initial request.

In Section 5, *"What is the actual process for responding to questions?"* you will identify the four specific behaviors required if you want to respond to questions in a way that allows you to build trust and rapport with your audience, critical to presentation success. You will discover what NOT to do by learning of a mistake made by the author of this guide.

In Section 6, *"When do you take questions…during or after your presentation?"* you will find help in considering the variables that will guide your decision.

In Section 7, *"Difficult people & challenging questions,"* you will discover how-to strategies for handling 30 specific situations most often mentioned in my training programs as being difficult to handle. You will find a variety of options for handling each situation. In some cases, you will receive specific wording to use; in other situations, you will be given behaviors to exercise. The most important feature of this section is the variety of options provided. Not all personalities are comfortable handling a given situation in exactly the same manner. Therefore, if one strategy feels uncomfortable, you can always select another. In most cases, the options are many and varied.

In Section 8, *"Summing up,"* you will read that being effective takes more than simple strategies; it takes the right character. This section looks at some of the personal qualities possessed by those who seem to be the most successful in making a positive impact on their audiences.

To get the most from this material requires that you become intimate with it. Keep this reference guide at your bedside, carry it in your briefcase, or put it in the top drawer of your desk. Whenever you have some time, take it out and review the contents, one section at a time. Take time to think about the attitude necessary for win/win encounters. Experience what it feels like to possess this attitude. Picture yourself inviting questions and listening with empathy. Hear yourself paraphrasing the audience's remarks, and responding in a polite, professional manner, regardless of what audience members may say.

At first, you may feel uncomfortable with strategies you are not accustomed to using. Over time, however, if practiced diligently, what is pictured in the mind, practiced on the lips, and felt in the heart becomes reality.

# ABOUT THIS REFERENCE GUIDE

# ABOUT THIS REFERENCE GUIDE

A question frequently asked in my Executive Speaking Skills course is, "How important is it to save time for questions?" My response is, "It is only important if you intend to accomplish your objectives."

An old Chinese proverb says, "I hear, I forget. I see, I remember. I participate, I do." Since the goal of most business presenters is to get people to *do* what you want them to *do*, active participation on the part of the audience is critical to presentation success.

*When you take the time to listen and respond to questions and comments from your audience, something quite wonderful happens. Communication takes place.*

When you take the time to listen and respond to questions and comments from your audience, something quite wonderful happens. Communication takes place. The speaker who only talks and never listens is not communicating with the audience; this person is simply performing, and rarely does performance alone sell.

Audiences, like individual members, need to be listened to, need to have their thoughts and feelings acknowledged, and need to have their questions and concerns answered. If you listen and respond with honesty and openness, you create a climate where trust is high and tension is low...important to opening closed minds and persuading people to take action.

*The question and answer session should not be left to chance.*

The question and answer session should not be left to chance. As an effective presenter you will want to prepare for it just as you prepare for the presentation itself.

That is why this book is practical. **It provides specific techniques for *The Art of Fielding Questions with Finesse*.** The dictionary defines *finesse* as "skill and adroitness in handling a difficult or highly sensitive situation." This book focuses on some of the most difficult and highly sensitive situations reported by my clients throughout the country.

**You will discover:**
1) how to prepare for a question and answer session,
2) how to elicit questions and comments, and
3) how to skillfully respond to the most difficult questions and/or people with finesse.

With desire, know-how, and practice, the question and answer portion of your presentation can be the event that sets the hook and compels your audience to say "YES" to your ideas!

Let us look at how it is done.

# WHY IS IT ADVISABLE TO ELICIT QUESTIONS AND/OR COMMENTS FROM YOUR AUDIENCE?

# WHY IS IT ADVISABLE TO ELICIT QUESTIONS AND/OR COMMENTS FROM YOUR AUDIENCE?

Most people live under the illusion of understanding. You may think that because you verbally expressed an idea, you were heard and understood by your audience. Not necessarily so.

*Information cannot flow into a closed vessel.*

Information cannot flow into a closed vessel. Two-way communication is critical in keeping open the channel between presenter and audience member. Research indicates that people tend to hear only about 25% of what is said, and remember even less. Therefore, it is possible that the audience did not hear your most convincing facts and figures. Even if they did hear, they may not agree with you. Whatever the case may be, **a well-handled question and answer session can provide many benefits.**

**It can:**

- ensure understanding

- let you know how the audience feels about you and/or your ideas

- clarify information

- provide an opportunity for you to fill in needed details

- acknowledge the audience and provide an opportunity for them to air their concerns

- give the audience a chance to exchange their ideas and viewpoints

- give you additional opportunity to sell your ideas

*...it pays to prepare...*

A mishandled question and answer session can undermine an otherwise excellent presentation. Therefore, it pays to prepare for it as you would your presentation.

# HOW DO YOU PREPARE FOR Q & A?

# HOW DO YOU PREPARE FOR Q & A?

A large utility company was receiving bad press. Several people from the company had been speaking on behalf of the company. Unfortunately, the press uncovered inconsistencies in the responses to the questions. Reporters were having a field day exposing the discrepancies on the front page of the local papers.

The company hired a high-priced consultant who offered a simple suggestion. He recommended that the company bring all of their spokespersons together for a brainstorming meeting. At that meeting they were to identify: 1) all the questions each of them had ever been asked, 2) all the questions they hoped nobody would ask, and 3) all the questions they wanted people to ask.

After the questions had been identified, he recommended that the company compile all the questions and the company's preferred responses to each question. Then, before anyone could speak on behalf of the company, that person had to be able to answer all the questions in a manner that demonstrated a clear understanding of company position.

The company followed the consultant's advice...and the results were favorable.

The same procedure can be helpful to the business presenter.

> **To prepare for the question and answer session, here is what you need to do:**
> 1) Identify all the questions that
>    a) you are sure will be asked,
>    b) you hope no one will ask, and
>    c) you want to be asked.
> 2) Prepare a response for each question.
> 3) Review your questions and the prepared responses several times prior to your presentation.
> 4) Ask someone from your organization to play the "devil's advocate" as a means of identifying any difficult questions you overlooked. Then, prepare a response for each.

After following these four steps, you will be prepared for the most difficult questions, and be ready for any opportunity to answer questions regarding information you could not cover in your more formal presentation.

Even if the audience does not ask the exact questions you have anticipated, I guarantee that, if you have done your homework, your responses will flow effortlessly, and you will look and sound in control of yourself and your material.

Once you are adequately prepared to respond to various questions, it is important that you create a climate that is "question friendly." The larger the audience, the more difficult it may be to get someone to "break the ice" by asking the first question. In that case, you will need to break the silence by eliciting comments and questions from the audience.

# HOW DO YOU ELICIT QUESTIONS?

# HOW DO YOU ELICIT QUESTIONS?

To encourage questions, set and maintain a tone of warmth and friendliness. It takes courage for many people to speak up in front of a group, especially since it means calling attention to themselves. Sometimes people are fearful of asking a "dumb" question, particularly in front of their peers or their superiors. If no questions are forthcoming, you will need to take the proactive approach of eliciting questions from the group. The following strategies usually produce the desired results.

*If you want questions, make your body language congruent with your words.*

• **Invite their questions.** How many times have you heard presenters ask, "Are there any questions?" while their heads are still stuck in their notes or while they are rifling through their transparencies? Lack of eye contact with members of your audience broadcasts a single message: "This is just a formality. I do not really want questions."

If you want questions, make your body language congruent with your words.

To send a message that says you genuinely want questions, try this three-step approach:

 • Step forward with your eyes on the audience, your arms open and your palms up when you ask the question as though inviting the audience to participate. Some people may find it more natural to use one hand and arm.

 • Ask, as you are stepping forward, "What questions might you have?" or "Who has the first question?" rather than, "Do you have any questions?" which implies a simple yes/no response. Open-ended questions like these assume that the audience will have questions.

 • After the invitation to ask a question, raise one hand into the air to indicate the way you would like the questions to be asked. Providing a method to ask questions makes it clearer to the audience how they are supposed to respond. Since audience members usually follow the leader, you should see a hand go up. If you do not, do not despair. There is still hope of getting interaction.

*Be sure to pause after you have asked for questions. Do not be afraid of silence.*

Be sure to pause after you have asked for questions. Do not be afraid of silence. People often need time to think of a way to formulate their questions. If, after five to ten seconds, there are still no questions, try the following.

• **Ask your own starter question.**  Say, "Something that I am often asked is..."  Then supply the answer.

• **Ask an open-ended question to the group.**  Let us say that you have been talking about a performance appraisal system.  You could say, "You have all encountered a similar system. What has been your experience?"  The open-ended question makes it easy for someone to respond as you are simply asking them to share their experience. Since there can be no right/wrong response to this kind of question, it does not pose a threat.  And because the phrasing requests a narrative response, the chances of getting something more than a yes/no response are good.

• **Bring up a topic on which you would like to elaborate.**  For example, "One area I barely touched on was the cross training we have initiated just recently.  I would be happy to elaborate on that if you would like."

• **Ask a direct question.**  Select someone you *know* would not be embarrassed or feel put on-the-spot by a question directed at them. Say, "Linda...what do you think?" or "Annette, I see you shaking your head..."

• **Ask a "Suppose" question.**  This is a good way to stimulate thinking and get them involved.  Say something like, "Suppose we were to... What do you think would happen?"  This might introduce a new idea or bring up a point you wanted to discuss but could not comfortably include in your presentation.

*It is easier to neutralize a written hostile comment or question than one submitted orally.*

• **Hand out cards and ask for written questions.**  This is usually best reserved for large audiences or for those situations where people would ask questions if they could remain anonymous. This also works well when the topic is controversial and you anticipate hostility. It is easier to neutralize a written hostile comment or question than one submitted orally.

• **Become the "devil's advocate."**  Say something controversial to stir the group up.

• **List the most commonly asked questions on a flip chart or over-head projector.**  These questions will usually spark questions from members of the audience.

*How you handle the questioner and respond to each question will be critical to your success.*

• **Announce your topic ahead of time and ask people to bring their questions.** This tactic is particularly good if you want your audience to begin thinking about your topic before the presentation. It allows people to formulate their questions without undue pressure, and it sends a strong signal that you will be expecting something from them.

• **Use humor...be playful.** Do this only if, 1) it is appropriate for the audience and 2) you are comfortable doing it. If both conditions exist, you could say, "I can play charades. Would that make it easier?" Keep a twinkle in your eye as you say it so you do not come across as insulting. You might also try, "I know that silence is golden. Shall we try for silver?"

• **As a final measure, hand out assignments.** Say, "Since there are no questions, I would like you each to do the following..." Then begin assigning actions to individual group members. This inevitably prompts a response from somebody.

I would recommend that you avoid the "planted" question as it usually comes off sounding "canned."

Of course, getting the questions rolling is only the beginning. How you handle the questioner and respond to each question will be critical to your success.

# WHAT IS THE ACTUAL PROCESS FOR RESPONDING TO QUESTIONS?

# WHAT IS THE ACTUAL PROCESS FOR RESPONDING TO QUESTIONS?

The process for responding to questions is easy, but it takes skill. Since most people do not naturally possess the skill, responding appropriately must be practiced faithfully and deliberately until it becomes natural.

**So what is the process?**

**Step 1: Give total attention.** This sounds basic, but it is not. Remember, as management guru Tom Peters says, "Perception is reality." Your body language plays an important role in determining whether or not a member of the audience feels heard.

*Tom Peters says, "Perception is reality."*

Too many times I have seen presenters pace the floor in front of the room, grunting, "uh-huh" "uh-huh" in quick succession, giving the impression that they are impatient with the questioner...that they already understand the question being asked. Sometimes presenters will actually interrupt the questioner and answer the question, sure that they have understood the question. When this happens, it is not uncommon for the questioner to say, "That is not what I was asking." The questioner ends up feeling unheard, the presenter looks foolish, and precious time is wasted.

*Avoid interrupting. Hear the questioner's complete question before you say anything.*

When someone asks a question, focus your eyes directly on the questioner. Move in slightly to get closer to the questioner. Your body might actually lean forward slightly. By nodding and providing expressions like, "uh-huh," "yes," we let the other person know we are focusing on what they are saying. In other words, everything about you should say, "I am listening." **Avoid interrupting. Hear the questioner's complete question before you say anything.**

People want acknowledgment, and giving your total attention is key.

**Step 2: Listen with your whole brain. Paraphrase the content and reflect any feelings.** *Looking* like you are listening is not enough. You must *really* listen. If you listen only for facts, you could be making a mistake. If you listen with your eyes, ears and heart, you are open to nuances and subtle emotional cues provided by the questioner. Feelings are sometimes more important than facts. In an emotionally charged situation, people need empathy.

*Looking like you are listening is not enough. You must really listen.*

The first task of our brain is to determine whether or not a situation is safe. All stimuli filter through the limbic system of the brain before they get to the part of the brain that actually *thinks*. What happens in the limbic area happens at an unconscious level. It is the part of our brain that simply *feels*. *Feeling* supersedes reason.

When a member of your audience is experiencing emotion, that person needs to feel that the environment is safe. Feeling safe often results from feeling understood. If you listen and attend only to the facts, that person is apt to feel unsafe in feeling emotion in your presence and become *more* emotional. Acknowledgment of feelings provides the *safety* needed. Only then can one get beyond feeling, to logic.

If your audiences are to trust you (trust being the foundation for any communication), you must be able and willing to get past your own thoughts and judgments. Once you do, your audience will know it by the way you respond with empathy and understanding. Then and only then can the gateway to understanding open.

Paraphrasing content and reflecting feeling is critical. It goes beyond simply restating the question. What can happen when one fails to do so adequately? An example follows.

A couple of years ago I was conducting a seminar in Detroit, Michigan. About 150 people were in the audience that day. The format was 20 minutes of lecture, 10 minutes of questions, followed by another 20 minutes of lecture. Just as I was closing the question and answer period, one more person raised his hand. I said, "Yes, sir. I will take one more question."

He responded, "I was in the Ionia State Prison the other day giving a presentation. One of the inmates started playing with my head, and he was giving off a very sensual message which made me extremely uncomfortable. How would you suggest that I have handled that?"

I said, "Let me make sure I understand. You were in the Ionia State Prison and one of the inmates was literally playing with your head?"

"Yes. And he was giving off a very sensual message that made me feel terribly uncomfortable. How should I have handled that?" he repeated.

Wanting to clarify further, I asked, "Where were you? Were you standing or sitting?"

"Sitting," he replied.

40

"And where was the inmate?" I asked.

"He was on the other side of the room."

At that point, I burst into laughter, along with the other 149 people in the room, with the words, "Oh, my, he must have had awfully long arms!"

The man jumped up and shouted, "No! No! You do not understand! That man was playing mind games by giving off very sensual body language that made me extremely uncomfortable. How should I have handled that?!"

Now, that was a different story. You see, I thought I had understood. I repeated his words back to him with the addition of the word "literally," thinking that he understood the word to mean the same as I did. Perhaps he did, but that repeat with an inclusion of the word "literally" did not do the job.

He saw me after the conference and told me that I had humiliated him in front of the group because I had made others laugh at him.

I told him that I was sorry, that that was not my intention. I thought I had understood and obviously I had not. I said I hoped he would forgive me.

If I had had a chance to replay that scene, rather than repeat his words, I would have paraphrased differently. "Let me make sure I understand. You mean that this inmate physically had his hands on the back of your head?" Then he could have clarified with, "Oh, no. He was playing mind games. He was standing across the room and his body language was very suggestive." I would have gotten a different picture. Unfortunately, the damage had been done.

**Learn from my mistake. Paraphrase, do not simply repeat. To repeat only guarantees that we have heard the words. It does not guarantee understanding.**

By failing to paraphrase, I caused the man embarrassment. It is probably accurate to say, he did not feel *safe* in my presence after that.

*Paraphrase, do not simply repeat.*

**The benefits gleaned from taking this second step are significant:**

1) It helps to guarantee your understanding.

2) It helps the audience to feel safe in your presence because they see you as a person who acknowledges and affirms others.

3) It makes sure that the audience has heard the question.

4) It gives you time to think of a response.

**Step 3: Give a bottom-line response.** Never give more than is needed. Keep your comments brief. If somebody asks which you prefer, a Macintosh or an IBM PC, do not give them the twenty reasons. Watch for body cues that tell whether or not you have provided enough information. If it is enough, you will probably see a nonverbal affirmation. If they need more, you are apt to see a questioning facial expression, chin-rubbing, or hesitancy in comments. Embellish with details only if you sense a real desire for more.

A turnoff to any audience is a presenter who uses the response to each question as an opportunity to give another speech. Do not do it. If you want questions to continue, keep your answers brief.

**Step 4: Remain in control.** If you are intent upon listening to the questioner, you will not get defensive. Defensiveness results when the need to protect self exceeds concern for the other.

A presenter with a defensive attitude can ruin an otherwise effective presentation. Once you get defensive, you leave the audience with negative feelings about you and, therefore, about your message. No matter how rude a member of the audience gets, never return with a rude answer. Remain calm and in control. You will add to your credibility, and the audience will continue to feel safe with you.

Knowing how to handle difficult people and challenging questions will add to your comfort and confidence. That is what the remainder of this little book of powerful techniques is all about.

*If you want questions to continue, keep your answers brief.*

*A presenter with a defensive attitude can ruin an otherwise effective presentation.*

*Remain calm and in control.*

42

# WHEN DO YOU TAKE QUESTIONS...DURING OR AFTER YOUR PRESENTATION?

# WHEN DO YOU TAKE QUESTIONS...DURING OR AFTER YOUR PRESENTATION?

Decide when you want questions. Announce your decision up front.

**If the topic is complex**, you may wish to allow for questions during the presentation to facilitate understanding throughout.

**If you have time constraints**, you may wish to hold questions until the end. Ask your audience, "Can we all agree to hold questions until the end?" If you get agreement, request that audience members write down any questions they have as you go along.

**Should you be interrupted after they have agreed to hold questions until the end**, you can remind them of their agreement. Another approach would be to provide a brief bottom-line answer, telling them that you will address their question later in your presentation and/or during Q & A.

**An alternative approach** would be to stop periodically throughout your talk and ask, "What questions do you have thus far?"

Once you have declared when you would like to entertain questions from the audience, it is important that you respond to each question with sensitivity, honesty, and directness. Let us look at how that is done.

*Respond to each question with sensitivity, honesty and directness.*

# DIFFICULT PEOPLE & CHALLENGING QUESTIONS

# DIFFICULT PEOPLE & CHALLENGING QUESTIONS

For years I have been asking my clients to list the most difficult people they encounter and the most challenging questions they get asked. The following are the most often mentioned. Not all require *finesse,* but all require skill.

*If one technique does not work, you can try another. Practice those that will work for you.*

You will note that some questions are accompanied by several suggestions for proper handling. Many of the ideas have been provided by participants in my training programs. The purpose of providing a smorgasbord of suggested responses is to offer you options. If one technique fails, you can try another. Practice those that will work for you.

Here goes.

*What do you do when the question is unclear or vague?* Although this question has already been alluded to earlier under *What is the Actual Process for Responding to Questions*, it is so frequently asked that the suggestions bear repeating.

- Listen. Paraphrase what you have understood as a means of seeking clarification. Avoid parroting their words, e.g. "Let me make sure I understand your question. You are asking me if _____?"

- If, after seeking clarification, you still do not understand, ask the questioner to give you an example or, if appropriate, to draw you a picture of what is meant. Say, "Could you give me an example to illustrate what you mean?"

*How do you avoid responding too quickly?* You can avoid a hurried, ill-advised response if you remember what has already been said about the critical listening step in the process.

- Paraphrase the question. After you have understood the question, simply pause and take time to think. Take a deep breath before you answer.

- If you are not comfortable with silence, after you have understood the question, ask for permission to take time to think. Say, "Let me think about that for a moment."

*Politeness and patience are the keys.*

**What do you do when the questioner speaks with a heavy accent or exhibits inappropriate language usage making it difficult for you to understand?** This situation is probably more prevalent today than ever before. Politeness and patience are the keys.

- Accept responsibility for not understanding and ask for what you want. For example, you might say, "I am having difficulty understanding. It would be helpful if you would ask your question again more slowly." Never put the responsibility for your not understanding on the questioner. Avoid saying things like, "Your accent is so thick, I cannot understand you."

- Ask for help from someone in the audience, e.g. "Can anyone help me with this question?"

- Ask the questioner to write the question on paper. Then be sure to express thanks for being patient with you. Say, "I am having difficulty understanding the question. Would you mind writing it on paper? I appreciate your patience with me."

**How do you deliver a negative response in a positive way?** Sometimes we cannot avoid being the bearer of bad news. If you have just announced bad news, such as budget cuts or plant closings, people are bound to be concerned. When the impact of your message stirs negative emotions in your audience, it is important that you are gentle and compassionate in your approach, and that you show empathy for them. However, it is also important that you remain as positive as possible.

**To remain positive, you may wish to try the following:**

- Recognize the positive aspects of the action to be taken. Focus on the ultimate good that will come from taking such action.

- Discuss the circumstances which led to the decision.

- Use clear and concise positive statements, leaving open any possible options for the future.

- State both the pros and cons of the action, always concluding with the pros which, hopefully, will outnumber the cons.

- Show empathy.  Show empathy.  Show empathy.

*Show empathy.*
*Show empathy.*
*Show empathy.*

*Be sure to maintain eye contact with the entire audience...*

**How do you avoid engaging in dialogue with a member of the audience to the exclusion of everyone else?** It is especially important that you know how to avoid getting into a situation where one person monopolizes the time allotted for Q & A.  The minute you engage in dialogue with one person, the rest of the audience feels excluded and may stop listening.  This is when side conversations are most apt to happen.

**The following strategy almost always eliminates the problem.**

- Be sure to maintain eye contact with the entire audience to avoid inviting dialogue with an individual member of the audience. Because the eyes control, it is important that you do not conclude your response to a question with your eyes resting on the questioner, but rather on another part of the audience. Then quickly follow-up with, "Who has the next question?"

- If the above fails, you may need to resort to a stronger measure  with something like, "George, I appreciate your interest in the topic.  I would like to hear what questions others have. Perhaps you and I could get together and talk afterwards."

**How do you handle a comment that had nothing to do with your objective?** No one needs to feel compelled to take time to discuss issues that do not relate to the topic under discussion.

- The most inoffensive technique is to give a brief response and redirect the topic to the original objective.

*Acknowledge the question and show appreciation.*

- Acknowledge the question and defer it to another time, e.g. "That question is certainly worthy of a response. Given our time constraints, I would like to restrict questions to the objectives for this meeting. Could we confer after the meeting to discuss that question further?" If you take time to write the question down, it will show your sincere interest in responding to the question.

- If not within the scope of your research, say so. "I am sorry, but that question is not within the scope of our study."

### How do you handle a question that will be answered later in your presentation?

- Give a quick bottom-line answer. Then say, "I will embellish this answer in a few minutes."

- Acknowledge the question and show appreciation. Then tell them the subject will be covered later. Also add, "If I forget, please remind me."

- Put the question on a flip chart and say, "I will be addressing this issue shortly." The act of writing the question down will show that you value their question and intend to answer it.

- Say, "You are thinking faster than I am talking. I will be getting to that soon."

### What do you do when the response needed is too technical for the majority of the audience?

- Offer a reference, such as, "The answer to that is complex. May I suggest that you read _____ for a more comprehensive discussion of that issue."

- Understand the question first. Then give a bottom-line response and tell them you would like to answer that more completely after the program, e.g. "The short answer to that question is _____. However, that does not provide the detail your question deserves. If you would like, we can discuss this in detail after the meeting."

### How do you handle a question covered in detail in your talk?

Be careful how you respond to this type of question. The tendency is to say something that will embarrass the questioner who apparently had not been listening, e.g. "I thought I had covered that point sufficiently in my talk." *Resist the temptation!* Embarrassing the questioner (who has already made himself look foolish) will only cause everyone to feel *unsafe* with you. After all, if you could embarrass one, you could embarrass others. Questions dry up when people perceive that they could be put down in front of their peers. Your credibility will suffer. Instead try the following.

- Say, "Let us revisit that point briefly." Make no attempt to invite the questioner to feel foolish for having asked the question.

- Simply give a brief response. Then say, "If you would like more detailed information, I would be happy to talk with you after the meeting."

### How do you handle a question when you do not know the answer?

As simple as this one seems, many people have difficulty with it. Remember, honesty is the best policy. Do not bluff. Your credibility is apt to suffer.

- Say, "I do not have that information, but I will get it and get back to you." Be sure you get back with a response in a timely manner.

- Ask for audience assistance in answering the question. Say, "Who might have a response to this question?"

- If you have an "expert" in the audience, defer the question to that person. Say, "Ed, you have expertise in this area. Would you mind answering that question?"

*Embarrassing the questioner will only cause everyone to feel unsafe with you.*

*Questions dry up when people perceive that they could be put down in front of their peers.*

*Do not bluff. Your credibility is apt to suffer.*

*Tell the truth*

**How do you determine when you have given enough information?**
Again, good advice bears repetition.

> - Seek clarification by paraphrasing the question. Once you know that you understand the intent of the questioner, respond to only what is asked. If additional information is requested, you will see the questioner's hand go up again or you will receive nonverbal cues such as a frown or a quizzical expression.

**How do you handle a request for proprietary information?**

> - Say, "I may be in a better position to comment on that particular issue at a later date once the information has been officially released."
>
> - Tell the truth. Say, "I am not at liberty to share that information at this time. It is proprietary."
>
> - Say, "I am not comfortable addressing that because of the nature of the information requested."
>
> - Say, "I could tell you, but then I would have to shoot you." This is an old military ploy. Better smile when you say it.

**How do you handle a situation when you cannot answer a question and the questioner will not accept the fact that you do not have an answer?** Some people want what they want when they want it. It is not always possible for you to provide it. Here's what you do.

> - Raise your voice (just a bit) and restate that you do not have that information, but you will get it and get back to them just as soon as possible, (or redirect to someone in the audience who has the information or can get it). You might say, "I do not have that information now, but I will get it and get back to you before 5:30 this afternoon."

54

Do not get trapped
into responding
without having the
facts.

- Plead an "Einstein." Say, "I appreciate your need for an immediate response. I am afraid that I must plead an 'Einstein.' I never keep information in my head that I can find somewhere else. As soon as I get it, I will get it to you." Then break eye contact with the questioner and move your eyes to the rest of the audience while asking, "What other questions might you have?"

**How do you handle a questioner whose personal experience refutes your facts?** This situation takes cool-headed thinking.

- Do not get trapped into responding without having the facts. Let us look at an example.

  **Question:** "How come I planted your hybrid XYZ and it only yielded 100 bushels? You told us that it should yield twice that much."
  **Response:** "Right now I am working with limited information. A number of factors affect the outcome. If I had access to more information, I could better respond."

**How do you handle a response from a superior who provides incorrect information?** This definitely takes finesse. How you handle this will depend upon the superior, your relationship with that person, and past experience.

- Stop and ask yourself:

  – How critical is it that this information be accurate **NOW?** If it is critical, you may want to say, "My understanding is different. Can we clarify before moving on?" If it is *not* important, you may choose to just ignore the error.

  – Who else is present? Is the boss's boss there? Sharing the information in private may be the best approach if accurate information is not critical to the meeting.

***How do you handle a person who answers for others?*** At times, when a member of your audience asks a question of another, a third party may interrupt to answer. Although these interruptions can be irritating, it is easy to rein in interrupters. These people are often over zealous in their desire to share what they know. Some do not even realize that what they are doing is inappropriate.

**To discourage the practice of answering for another member of the audience, try the following:**

- Thank the interrupter for the point of view; then turn to the person who was asked the question and request input. Say, "Thank you, Bob." Then turn to Susan (the person who was asked the question) and say, "Susan, how would you respond to that question?"

- Ignore the person who answers and maintain your attention on the one who was asked the question and wait for the response.

- Politely say, "Excuse me, Bob, but I would like to hear what Susan has to say about that."

**To keep your poise when they interrupt and answer the question for you, do the following:**

- If you concur with their response, simply say so or give another perspective.

- If their answer was a good one, check with the questioner to see if they are satisfied with the response.

- If the person does this more than once, politely interrupt by saying something like, "Excuse me. I would like to respond to that question." Then clarify the question and respond.

***How do you handle a person who interprets for others?*** This person is "related" to the person who answers for others. It is the person who says after every comment or question, "What John is trying to say is…" When you encounter this person, try the following.

- Turn to the person who made the initial comment and ask if the interpreter's restatement was accurate. If you do this every time the situation happens, it should not take long before the interpreter gets the point and stops his annoying behavior.

- Quickly interrupt the interpreter with something like, "Excuse me, Ed, but I would like to see if I have a clear understanding of what Susan is asking."

***How do you deal with the "funnel"...the person who serves as the mouthpiece for all others in attendance?*** In union or work group environments, you will sometimes find one person who serves as the spokesperson for everyone else. All questions will come from this person. If you would like more of a discussion with many involved, you will need to find a way of getting around the "mouthpiece" to those with the questions.

- Solicit participation from others by saying, "I need clarification of that question from the person who has the need to know."

- Interview participants ahead of time and ask for their questions then. Address them at the meeting.

- Limit the number of questions per person up front.

- Ask them to write out their questions so they can be read.

- Ask questions of a particular person, e.g. "Joe, what do you think?"

- Acknowledge the situation. Identify the spokesperson. Say, "It appears that John is serving as your spokesperson. If that is the case, I will respond to your questions as posed by him. However, should anyone wish for clarification or expansion on anything I say, please let me know."

***How do you respond to a "loaded" question?*** The person who asks this kind of question usually has a desire to embarrass you. The question is no-win. It is a question that cannot be answered, e.g. "When did you stop beating your wife?" Responding to a "loaded" question takes skill.

*Control your body language. Remain open. Maintain good eye contact with the questioner during the question.*

- Control your body language. Remain open. Maintain good eye contact with the questioner during the question. Avoid arm crossing and hands-on-hips defiance. Listen closely for the "underlying message." Avoid getting trapped into responding directly. Moving your eyes to the rest of the audience, simply provide a statement that expands the "trap" question or exposes a faulty premise.

  **Question:** "Is it black or white?"
  **Response:** "The entire spectrum is under consideration."

  **Question**: "Since drug companies have caused the healthcare crisis, why not just nationalize the drug industry?"
  **Response:** With your eyes on the audience, say, "I cannot accept the premise that drug companies caused the healthcare crisis, so I am unable to respond to that question." Looking to another part of the room, quickly move on with, "Who else has a question?"

- Turn the tables. Ask, "That is an interesting question, Mike. What do you think?" Caution: It would be easy to lose your focus, depending on the response to your question. Be sure to keep your objective for the meeting in mind.

*Separate the questions and address each issue individually.*

***How do you handle a complex question?*** This is a question composed of several questions.

**If you hear multiple questions:**

- Separate the questions and address each issue individually. Say, "You have asked three questions. I would like to address each separately. I will begin with the first question..."

- If time is limited and you would like others to have a chance to get their questions answered, you may wish to say, "You have asked a series of questions. Which part would you like me to address?"

- If you are being bombarded by questions from several people before you are able to respond to any of them, say, "I am hearing several questions." Restate the questions you heard…and then say, "First, I will take Joe's question, then Jane's, then Ed's and Susan's." Then answer each in turn.

**How do you handle a "What if" question?** Do not get trapped into speculation. When someone asks you a hypothetical question, take a positive approach.

- Discuss the factors surrounding the issue on which a decision would have to be based.

- Simply state what *is* and what the positive expectations *are*. The following is an example.

**Question**: What if they close our plant down?
**Response:** Right now there is no discussion of closing this plant. We are anticipating a healthy economic forecast.

**Question:** What if this new system does not work?
**Response:** We have spent months studying the system. We are confident that it will do what we need it to do.

**How do you respond to a question that requires you to take a position with which you do not agree or a position that is not "politically correct?"** Sometimes you may be required to support unpopular organization decisions. No need to fret.

- Simply state, "My personal opinion is not an issue here."

- Acknowledge the differing views. Reiterate that the chosen path is considered best for the organization as a whole. Outline the decision process.

- Say, "While the decision is not my first choice, I believe it is valid and workable, and I am committed to making it successful."

- Do not give your opinion. Instead say, "This is the direction our organization is going, and I support the organization."

*Keep the audience focused on the reason they are there...*

**How do you answer when there is no "right or wrong" to the issue?** Sometimes the point of the meeting is simply to air views, not to determine which "solution" is the best. Keep the audience focused on the reason they are there, and allow no one to discredit another's point of view.

- State up front that there is no definitive answer. You are simply there to air all views...not to pass judgment.

- Do not accept ownership of any one point of view. Serve strictly as facilitator, not leader or participant. Simply allow all points of view to be heard.

*How do you avoid a gripe session?* The key to handling this is not to allow it to happen in the first place.

- Ask for proactive suggestions. Say, "Rather than focusing on what is not possible, let us focus on what we can change. What suggestions for positive action might you have?"

*Recognize that experts want to be given credit for what they know.*

*How do you handle the "expert" who wants to editorialize?* Recognize that experts want to be given credit for what they know.

- Acknowledge them and what they have said, agree where you can, and then add to their information. Thank them.

- Simply thank them and acknowledge a good point. Move on.

*Whatever you do, come prepared with more than your opinion.*

- Ask for their help **ahead of time.** Tell them that you recognize their expertise and during your presentation you would like to call on them for their opinion when you make reference to _____ . They will not need to editorialize if they know you plan to call on them as experts. Tell the audience up front that you have an expert in the group (give the person's name) and tell them that you will be calling on the expert for comment as you discuss certain issues.

*How do you handle the "know-it-all"?* A know-it-all is usually a person who comes armed with "the facts" gained as a result of advanced degrees, position in the organization, or length of experience. With this person you must stick to the facts. A know-it-all likes to be positioned as the authority on the subject. Whatever you do, come prepared with more than your opinion.

- Make sure that your facts are documented. You cannot be too prepared for this person.

- Relate *your* experience. People cannot refute what happened to you.

- Come prepared with quotes by recognized authorities in the field that support your evidence.

- Tell the audience up front that you and the know-it-all do not agree. State the know-it-all's case. Then tell why you do not agree.

- If they provide information that contradicts yours, say, "You may be right about that. Let me share my research with you." Then share it. With the words, "You may be right about that," comes the implied message, "You may also be wrong about it." Because of the way it is stated, you have given your opponent nothing to push against and you can refute the argument with well-documented facts.

- As with the expert, ask for the know-it-all's help before the presentation. What initially may appear to be strong opposition can become, with a little finesse on your part, support for your position.

***How do you handle a loud, disruptive detractor?*** This person attempts to dominate, talks too loudly, and will not shut up. The comment usually adds little or nothing to the discussion; it simply derails it. Sometimes, invading the detractor's space both physically and with your eyes is enough to quiet the interruption. When it is not, other measures are needed.

- Try turning your back on the detractor. Avoid making eye contact. Unfortunately, these people are difficult to ignore, but the less attention given them, the better. If detractors wave their hands to be called on, do not see them.

- If you have called on them and they go into a monologue, interrupt them with the question, "And your point is...?"

- Say, "I need your help." Then ask them if they would take notes or list follow-up "to do's"...anything to keep them busy.

- Call a time out. Then approach this person and ask for help. Tell the detractor that you have a limited amount of time to respond so you would appreciate help in keeping discussion to a minimum. Offer thanks for cooperation. Suggest the two of you meet privately to discuss the issue.

*Everyone has a right to disagree with you.*

***How do you handle someone who disagrees or who wants to discredit you or your information?*** Everyone has a right to disagree with you. In fact, disagreement can be a positive if it exposes holes in your argument and forces you to present convincing evidence to support your case. The person who attempts to discredit you or your information, however, is a different story. Each is handled with a different approach.

*Do your homework.*

**Let us begin by taking a look at the person who simply disagrees.**

- Do your homework.  If you have done proper audience analysis, you should have an idea going into the presentation what other points of view exist.  Allow this information to work for you. Early in your prepared remarks, you can mention that  some disagree with your proposal, that opposing points of view exist. If you summarize the opposing views in the context of your material, you not only build credibility for yourself, but you take the wind out of  the opposition's sails and thus the sting out of any comments that they might wish to make.

- If your desire is to convince those who disagree with you, even after your presentation, you may wish to try the following formulas:

1) Practice the 3-F's.

***Feel*** – Reflect the feeling they are experiencing.
***Felt*** – Let them know they are not alone.
***Found*** – Tell them what others have discovered from "buying" your message. Here you would provide convincing facts.

**Feel:**
"I understand your **feeling** of concern."
**Felt:**
"You are not alone.  Other people have **felt** exactly the same way as you do."
**Found:**
"But what they **found** was that they had nothing to worry about. We have customers who have had their water beds now for over 10 years and they have never had a leak in their mattresses or their systems."

2) Try the 4-C's approach.

***Clarify*** – Give a listening response to make sure you have understood the remark.
***Concede*** – Find a point of agreement and say so.
***Convince*** – Make a statement or ask a question with which they can agree.
***Close*** – This is what you propose.

**Clarify:**
"It sounds like you think it will be too costly to redecorate the front offices?" (yes)
**Concede:**
"I agree. It will take adequate funding."
**Convince:**
"Would you agree that first impressions are important?" (yes)
**Close:**
"That is exactly why I think we should spend the money to redecorate. The first thing our customers see when they come into our building is the front offices. Because they are still decorated in gold and avocado, the look of the early 1960s, we look dated. If our offices look dated, people will assume that our practices are dated, too. Therefore, we need to look like we have ushered in the 90s by presenting an up-to-date image. Redecorating is good business."

You get the idea. With both of the above strategies, you begin where the other person is FIRST, and then you lead them to where you want them to go.

- Clarify their position first. Then, without using either of the words "but" or "however," simply restate your position and the evidence that proves your point. Do not "disagree." State what you have discovered. Say, "From my experience (or research), I have discovered..."

- Sometimes you may need to "agree to disagree" when it is simply a matter of opinion.

- Thank them for their point of view and ask others for their opinions...or simply move on. No need to even comment.

*Sometimes you may need to "agree to disagree"...*

**If someone personally attacks you or attempts to discredit your information, another approach is recommended.**

- Someone says, "Your research stinks!" This is an attack on both you and the material you have presented. It is also vague criticism. In a case like this, simply turn the tables and say, "What is it specifically about my research that you find inaccurate?" This forces them to get specific. If they cannot, they do not have a leg to stand on. They know it, and so does the rest of the audience. If they can get specific, you can then refute with appropriate evidence.

- Someone says, "You are lying!" There is a point at which we can "draw the line." This is one of those instances. A simple unemotional response of "No, I am not lying," followed by a reiteration of the facts with your eyes on the rest of the audience should handle this.

- Be prepared so you can quietly and decisively refute the accusation with evidence and quoted recognized sources of authority. Begin by saying, "I have data to support these results."

- Ask for support from someone else in your audience who shares your position.

*How do you handle an attack on the organization?* How you handle this will probably depend on whether or not the attack is justified.

- If the accusation is accurate, show understanding and empathy...then point to positive steps that the company is taking.

**Question:** "Your company was negligent in its packaging, making it easy for some kook to tamper with it."
**Response:** "You are right. Our packages were not tamperproof. However, we have learned from our experience. We have recalled and removed all defective packaging, and we are taking every measure to guarantee future product safety. We are confident that this will never happen again."

...the "Yes, but"
game... is a trap...

- If it is not justified, defend the organization. Say, "That is not true." Overcome the objections with factual information.

- (See the 3-F Strategy, page 63).

***How do you handle the person who gives a "Yes, but" response to your response?*** In his book, The Games People Play, Psychiatrist Eric Berne analyzed the "Yes, but" game. It is a trap that you do not want to fall into. "Yes, but" is simply another way of saying, "I let you talk, but now I am going to explain the way it really is." Refuse to play the game.

- Ask, "What do YOU recommend?"

- Say, "It sounds as if you already have some firm beliefs that perhaps you would like to share."

- Say, "That is something to consider. What do others think?"

Above all, do not keep bantering back and forth. It is a no-win proposition.

***How do you deal with an angry person?*** Let your experience in dealing with angry people be your guide. You have undoubtedly learned that certain behaviors do NOT work with angry people.

- *Do not* respond in kind. Do not get angry back.

- *Do not* refuse to acknowledge their feelings. For example, do not say, "You should not feel that way."

- *Do not* attempt to belittle them with sarcasm before the group.

- *Do not* blame someone else.

- *Do not* dismiss their remarks as insignificant.

A universal truth is, "Acceptance and/or agreement opens a person's mind. Disagreement and/or non-acceptance closes a person's mind." As you can see, the above responses do not work with an angry person because each response invites a closed mind through disagreement and/or nonacceptance.

- Be sure the angry person remains sitting. According to an MIT study, it is more difficult for people to remain angry if they are sitting down. Stay in control yourself. Be aware of your body language. Move closer. Lean forward slightly. Send signals that reach out and draw the other person to you. Absolutely DO NOT attempt to explain your point of view at this time. Remember, an emotionally charged person's ability to reason is blocked.

Listen closely to what the angry person is saying. Avoid taking the anger personally. You may simply be the person with whom the angry party has chosen to vent. Remember, listening with empathy does not imply agreement. It simply suggests that you care enough to hear their views.

Paraphrase content. Reflect feeling. Do not let them go on and on and on. When they pause for a breath, interject a listening response. Say, "Let me see if I understand what you are angry about. You are angry because..." Even an angry person will listen when someone is attempting to understand. Each listening response releases pressure, like slowly letting the air out of an inflated balloon. With each response, a bit more of the air is released, until eventually, the balloon is deflated.

If you do not agree with the angry person, try a tactful way of letting that person know without actually saying, "You are wrong." You might say, "I would be angry, too, if I thought that was happening." It is a matter of validating the other's feelings that is important. Validating feelings and understanding the facts are keys to opening closed minds. Once people have been heard, they are usually more receptive to hearing you when you say, "Let me share with you why that action was taken."

"Resolving conflict is rarely about who is right. It is about acknowledgement and appreciation of differences."

*–Thomas Crum, The Magic of Conflict*

*...when the topic is controversial, the presenter must exercise good facilitation skills.*

The better the listener you are, the less reluctant people will be to share even their negative views with you. The benefits are many: greater trust in you, less back-biting, and more information at your disposal. In addition, you will be serving as a positive role model for others who observe your behavior.

Once the angry person has been heard, and you have had a chance to state the "why" of your position, you may even wish to ask that person for solutions for improvement. The greater their involvement, the less need they have for continuing anger.

If the person turns out to be a totally unreasonable person, you will discover it soon enough.

Two concepts to remember:
1) **What you resist will persist.**
2) **Never give anybody anything to push against.**

Sincere "active" listening is much like the martial art of Aikido. You remain relaxed and in control and deflect the energy of your attacker from you in such a way that the conflict becomes you and the attacker against the problem.

Thomas Crum, in his book The Magic of Conflict, says it best when he states, "Resolving conflict is rarely about who is right. It is about acknowledgement and appreciation of differences."

*How do you handle a situation that appears to be getting out of control?* When a topic generates a great deal of interest, or when the topic is controversial, the presenter must exercise good facilitation skills. However, if you find yourself in a situation where the audience seems to be taking over the meeting, a number of options are available.

- Make a comment like, "It seems we have a lot of interest in the subject; let us refocus our attention on..."

- Pause, stand quietly, wait...continue when you have their attention. Silence can be a powerful attention getter.

*Should two or more members of your audience get into a conflict, act to prevent escalation...*

- Look at the most obvious detractors. Ask if they have any questions...OR...directly ask one of them a question.

- Project your voice...OR...speak more softly. Move toward the offenders.

- Get the audience involved in another way, e.g. "I would like you to get together with the person next to you and take three minutes to brainstorm ways that we might ...."

- Ask for a time out or take a break.

***How do you break up an audience in conflict?*** This is similar to the above in that you have temporarily lost control of the meeting. Controversial topics inevitably bring an emotional response from some people. Should two or more members of your audience get into a conflict, act to prevent escalation or you risk losing complete control.

- Ask for attention. Say, "Mike! Tom! May I have your attention." Then, calmly request that the people in conflict take an uninterrupted opportunity to present their viewpoints. Once they have done so, summarize your understanding of each viewpoint. Acknowledge the difference of opinion. Suggest that, in keeping with time available and the objectives for your meeting, you would like to move forward. Suggest that perhaps they would like to take up the discussion at another time.

- Use humor, e.g. "If you cannot see the validity of each other's opinions, I have a set of boxing gloves you might like to use outside." Smile when you say this.

**How do you regain control once you have completely lost the attention of the group?** Unfortunately, no matter how much control you exhibit with your eyes (see above strategy), sometimes the topic is such a stimulating one, people are not always inclined to want to wait to hear others out. If two or three people talking has escalated to a general fray, assertive measures must be taken.

*If two or three people talking has escalated to a general fray, assertive measures must be taken.*

- Call "TIME OUT!"

- Take a break.

- Depending on the length of time the meeting has been in progress, you may wish to conclude the meeting.

- Try theatrics, e.g. tap dance, throw a nerf ball at someone, etc. (This can only be done by someone willing to risk looking silly.)

- Get SILENT. Simply SMILE. (This indicates in a pleasant way, "We have mayhem and need to get under control.")

- Try the GONG SHOW approach. If the meeting is a standing weekly/monthly meeting, anticipate the control problem and establish an audio indicator, such as a GONG that by its sound alone announces, "You are out of line. Let us get quiet."

- If you can identify a ringleader, speaking loudly, ask that person a direct question, "Ed! What do you think we should do?"

- Break the audience into small groups. Give them a specific question to consider. Set a time limit, such as three minutes.

*Out of respect for other presenters, no one presenter should ever take more than the allotted time.*

*...make it clear up front how long you will address questions.*

***How do you end the Q & A period gracefully?*** Question and answer periods can become painful for both the audience and the presenter if the presenter does not know how to call it quits. A well-run meeting usually has a starting and ending time. Only on rare occasions should a meeting run overtime more than a few minutes.

When you are one of several presenters on a program, it is imperative that you know exactly how much time you have. Out of respect for other presenters, no one presenter should ever take more than the allotted time. It is inexcusable to force another presenter to shorten his remarks because a previous speaker chose to take extra time.

For the comfort of everyone concerned, make it clear up front how long you will address questions.

- Set a time limit for discussion. For example, say something like, "I will take the next 15 minutes to respond to your questions. Who has the first question?"

- Use a timekeeper.

- When you can see that time is running short, say, "We have just enough time for two more questions."

- Refer to a later date and time. Say, "Our time is up. If you still have issues that need to be addressed, see me after the program and we can set a time to meet and discuss your questions."

- If the discussion is important to only certain members of your audience, provide an opportunity for those who want and/or need to leave to do so. Then you can continue the discussion with those remaining.

**Remember**:

A question and answer session can be the most stimulating part of your meeting. It is imperative, however, that you keep a few key points in mind.
- Be prepared.
- Maintain a proactive attitude.
- Respect the views of others.
- Listen with understanding and empathy.

A positive attitude and good communication skills, along with a well-prepared presentation, will go a long way in guaranteeing success.

# SUMMING UP

# SUMMING UP

From having worked with thousands of individuals over the past several years, it has become clear to me that those who make the greatest positive impact on others recognize a basic truth: *What you communicate is what comes back to you.*

Successful presenters exhibit a recognition of this truth through certain attitudes and behaviors.

• All stand before their audience *prepared.* They not only understand the value of their message to the audience, but they communicate it clearly and succinctly. They respect their audience's time.

• All seem to understand that others want to be persuaded, but only through honest, open interaction.

• All recognize that differing viewpoints exist, and they welcome discussion of those differences.  They do not force their ideas on anyone. Through open discussion of facts, evidence, and experience, they work with the group to influence  them positively.

• All demonstrate the attitude that others are worthy and valuable. They listen; they do not pass judgment. They restate or enhance their own views only after they have taken the time to understand the views of others.

• All are open to learning from their audience.  They view others as teachers. When someone provides them with information or a perspective of which they were unaware, they show appreciation.

• All begin where people *are*, rather than where they want them to *be.* They recognize how important it is for people to be affirmed for what they *know* and *understand.*

Personal integrity and genuine respect for others is critical to your success as a presenter. Once you combine those with a mastery of the strategies found in this book, you will have discovered the secret to *The Art of Fielding Questions with Finesse.*

*What you communicate is what comes back to you.*

*Personal integrity and genuine respect for others is critical to your success as a presenter.*

# ABOUT THE AUTHOR

**Mary Jane Mapes, CSP**

is an internationally known communication consultant, trainer and professional speaker. She blended a Master's degree in communication with her experiences as a radio personality, as a goodwill ambassador for the National Cherry Industry and as an educator/trainer with over 20 years experience. Her expertise includes effective business communication, persuasive presentations, listening, and customer service. Her advice and training is sought by such organizations as The Upjohn Company, IBM, James River Corporation, Owens Corning, Avon Products, Inc., The American Association of Occupational Health Nurses, and numerous hospitals and healthcare organizations throughout the United States.

Mary Jane is past president of her local chapter of the American Society for Training and Development, past president of the Professional Speakers Association of Michigan, a member of the National Speakers Association, and is one of only a small number of women worldwide to have earned the prestigious Certified Speaking Professional designation granted by the National Speakers Association for standards of excellence in the field of speaking. She is author of a videotape training program on effective communication which is distributed internationally, video and audio cassette learning albums, a quarterly newsletter, *The Communication Connection*, and numerous published articles on the subject of communication. Mary Jane presents over 100 seminars and speeches annually.

# Order Form

Mary Jane Mapes & Associates
7735 Angling Road
Kalamazoo, MI 49024
(616) 324-1847 • FAX (616) 324-1848 • (800) 851-2270

## $15.00 (U.S.) per book
### *Price discounts on volume orders available.*

*The Art of Fielding Questions with Finesse* ____copies @ $_____each $_____total book cost

Shipping & Handling  $_____
($3.50 for the first book and $.50 for each additional book)
Michigan Res. 6% tax $_____

TOTAL $_____

Please send Purchase Order, Check or Money Order to:  **Mary Jane Mapes & Associates**
**7735 Angling Road**
**Kalamazoo, MI 49024**

To place orders, call toll free (800) 851-2270 or drop your order in the mail using this order form.  Orders may also be faxed to (616) 324-1848.  With mailed or faxed orders, please include your Purchase Order number. ***All orders except those with a P.O.# must be prepaid.***

## Ship to:

Name_____

Job Title_____

Organization_____

P.O. Box_____

Street Address_____

City/State_____Zip_____

Country_____

Phone (      )_____ PO#_____

*Allow four to six weeks for delivery.*